What to Cook When You're Tired of Everything

A Cookbook For The Busy Family

Book cover by Cari Anderson

Illustrations by Cari Anderson

Editing and graphic design by Lori Krustchinsky

Edition 1 2024

A LETTER FROM CARI

Welcome to my cookbook! I'm so excited to share these delicious recipes that I have made for my family and friends.

Do you ever get tired of cooking the same things over and over for dinner? Do you feel overwhelmed with deciding what dish to take to a gathering? If so, this cookbook is for you! I have put together a collection of many different recipes for all occasions.

My love for cooking started as a child in my grandmother Didi's kitchen. It has continued on into adulthood and now it is something I love sharing with my own family. I hope you enjoy these recipes, and they bring happiness to you and your family.

With lots of love,

Cari

CONTENTS

CONTENTS

CONTENTS

CONTENTS

CONTENTS

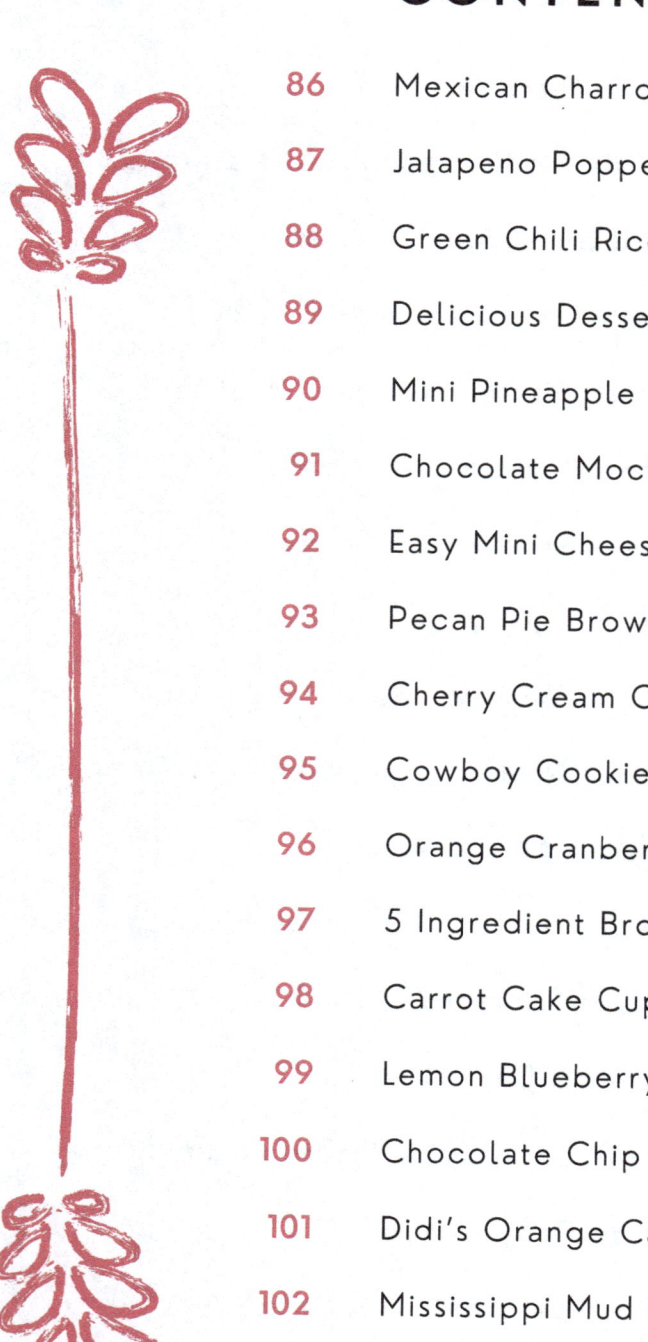

Appetizers

FRIED PICKLE RANCH DIP

I love pickles and I love Ranch! Together they make the perfect combination for a delicious dip.

INGREDIENTS

8 ounces of cream cheese

1 cup sour cream

1 packet of Ranch seasoning

1 cup pickles chopped

1 garlic clove minced

3/4 cup Panko bread crumbs

1 Tbs olive oil

1/4 tsp salt

DIRECTIONS

Mix together the cream cheese, sour cream, Ranch seasoning, pickles, and garlic.

Add 1 Tbs olive oil to a pan and heat. Add in Panko breadcrumbs and toast them for around 5 minutes until golden brown. Stir in the salt with the breadcrumbs. Sprinkle breadcrumbs over the dip and serve cold.

PUFF PASTRY SAUSAGE ROLLS

These sausage rolls are one of my favorite things to make when hosting a party. They are so easy and quick to make. Serve these at any get together and they will be one of the first foods gone!

INGREDIENTS

2 Puff pastry sheets

2 links of sausage

1/4 cup melted butter

1/2 tsp salt

DIRECTIONS

Preheat your oven to 400 degrees and thaw out the puff pastry sheet. Once thawed, roll the puff pastry sheet around the sausage link. Add a little bit of water to the seam of the puff pastry and pinch together so the puff pastry will stick together. Brush melted butter all over the puff pastries and sprinkle a little bit of salt on top. Place in a baking pan lined with parchment paper and bake for 20 minutes.

TIPS

You can find Puff pastry sheets in the freezer section of your grocery store.

TOMATO TARTLETS

Serve these beautiful tomato tartlets at lunch, brunch, or as an appetizer before dinner. They will look like you've spent a lot of time making them when in fact they are very simple and easy to make!

INGREDIENTS

1 sheet of puff pastry

8 ounces ricotta cheese

1/4 cup grated parmesan cheese

1 egg

1/2 pound cherry tomatoes sliced in half

1 tsp salt

1 tsp pepper

1 tsp garlic powder

1 tsp oregano

1 Tbs olive oil

DIRECTIONS

Preheat your oven to 425 degrees. Cut the puff pastry sheet into 6 rectangles. Mix together ricotta cheese, parmesan cheese, salt, pepper, garlic powder, and oregano. Spoon cheese mixture onto puff pastry, leaving some space on the edges. Top with tomatoes. Brush the tomatoes with olive oil. Whisk the egg and brush the edges of the puff pastry with the egg. Bake for 20 minutes.

NANA'S CUCUMBER DIP

My mother-in-law makes this delicious dip for Easter every year. It is absolutely amazing and I can eat it year round!

INGREDIENTS

2 - 8 ounces packages cream cheese softened

1 cucumber peeled, seeds removed and grated

1 red onion chopped

1 cup miracle whip

2 tsp lemon juice

1/4 tsp salt

DIRECTIONS

Mix everything together and serve cold.

BUTTER PECAN HAVARTI BITES

Everyone will think you're a gourmet chef when you serve these. They're buttery, sweet, and creamy and will be the highlight of the meal.

INGREDIENTS

30 mini phyllo shells

8 ounces Havarti cheese

3 Tbs butter melted

4 Tbs brown sugar

1/2 cup chopped pecans

DIRECTIONS

Place phyllo shells on a baking sheet. Cut up cheese into small pieces and place into phyllo shells. Melt butter in a pan and add in brown sugar. Stir until brown sugar is dissolved. Add in pecans and stir. Spoon pecan mixture over the cheese into the shells. Bake at 350 for 8-10 minutes.

SUMMER CORN DIP

There is nothing better than eating this dip with tortilla chips on a hot summer day. This is a great dip to take to a BBQ. You will be sure to impress the guest!

INGREDIENTS

15 ounce can of corn

22 ounces of Mexicorn

1 cup sour cream

1 cup mayo

1 bundle of green onions chopped

2 cups shredded cheese

Salt and pepper to taste

DIRECTIONS

Mix everything together and serve cold. Store in the refrigerator.

EASY SHRIMP CEVICHE

This is a wonderful dish to serve during the summer. It's cool, light, and refreshing and perfect for a hot day.

INGREDIENTS

12 ounces cooked shrimp

2 Roma tomatoes

1/2 red onion chopped

2 jalapenos chopped

1/2 bunch green onion chopped

1/4 cup cilantro

1/2 cup lime juice

1/4 tsp salt

DIRECTIONS

Cut up the shrimp into small bite size pieces.
Chop the tomatoes, onion, jalapenos, green onion, and cilantro into small pieces.
Squeeze lime juice on top and add salt. Mix together.
Serve cold.

.

CHICKEN TACO PINWHEELS

I love making these pinwheels when I am taking a dish to a party. They are always a crowd favorite.

INGREDIENTS

12 ounces cream cheese

1/2 cup sour cream

2 Tbs taco seasoning

1 can Rotel

2 cups cooked shredded chicken

1/2 tsp salt

1/2 tsp garlic powder

1 1/2 cup shredded cheese

8 tortillas

DIRECTIONS

Mix all ingredients together and spread mixture onto tortillas. Roll up tortillas and cut into slices.

TIPS

Refrigerate for at least one hour before slicing.

19

CLASSIC BRUSCHETTA

This is an easy and delicious Italian appetizer. The toasted bread with fresh ingredients to top it make for the perfect crowd pleaser.

INGREDIENTS

1 French loaf

Olive oil for brushing

1 garlic clove sliced in half

7 Roma tomatoes

1/4 cup chopped white onion

1/4 chopped basil

2 tsp balsamic vinegar

1 tsp minced garlic

1/4 tsp pepper

DIRECTIONS

Preheat oven to 400 degrees. Cut French loaf into slices. Brush both sides of bread with olive oil and sprinkle with salt. Bake for 5 minutes on each side. Once done, rub garlic clove on 1 side of bread.

Tomato mixture: Chop tomatoes and onion. Add in basil, balsamic vinegar, minced garlic, salt and pepper. Top bread with tomato mixture.

JALAPENO POPPER DIP

INGREDIENTS

8 ounces cream cheese

1/2 cup sour cream

1 packet Ranch seasoning

1 (3 ounce) pack of real bacon bits

4-5 jalapenos seeded and chopped

1 cup shredded cheese

DIRECTIONS

Mix together the cream cheese, sour cream, and Ranch seasoning until smooth. Add in the chopped jalapenos, bacon bits, and shredded cheese and mix until combined. Refrigerate.

TIPS

Set the cream cheese out to soften before mixing. If you would like the dip spicy, leave some of the jalapeno seeds in.

MEXICAN SAUSAGE BALLS

I love sausage balls and have been making them for years. This recipe is a step up from a plain sausage ball and is perfect to serve for any occasion.

INGREDIENTS

16 ounces pork sausage

8 ounces cream cheese

1 1/2 cup Bisquick

1 packet Taco seasoning mix

1 1/2 cup shredded cheese

DIRECTIONS

Preheat oven to 400 degrees. Mix all of the ingredients until well combined. Roll into 1 inch balls. Bake for 20 minutes.

TIPS

Use hot pork sausage if you would like spicier sausage balls. Use a stand mixer for easier mixing.

SALSA VERDE

INGREDIENTS

10-15 tomatillos

3 jalapenos

1/2 onion

4 cloves garlic

2 Tbs olive oil

1/4 cup water

2 Tbs chicken boullion

1 tsp salt

1 bunch cilantro

DIRECTIONS

In a large pan, heat olive oil and add in tomatillos, jalapenos, onion, and garlic. Cook for 5-10 minutes until vegetables are soft. Pour vegetables into a blender. Then add in water, chicken bouillon, salt, and cilantro into the blender. Blend and refrigerate.

Soup, Stews, and more

THE BEST CHILI

Serves 6-7

This is my favorite chili recipe, and I have made a lot of them! I make this for the first cold front of the year and multiple times throughout fall and winter.

INGREDIENTS

2 pounds ground beef

1 tsp salt

1 tsp pepper

2 packets of chili seasoning

3 cloves minced garlic

2 Tbs Worcestershire sauce

2 bell peppers chopped

1 onion chopped

2 Tbs tomato paste

1 (15 ounce) can crushed tomatoes

3 cups beef broth

DIRECTIONS

In a large pot, brown ground beef and season with salt and pepper. Add in packets of chili seasoning and Worcestershire sauce. Add bell peppers, onion, and garlic. Cook for 5 minutes until vegetables are soft. Stir in tomato paste and crushed tomatoes. Pour in beef broth. Bring to a boil. Reduce heat, cover and simmer for 30 minutes.

EASY POZOLE

Serves 4-6

INGREDIENTS

3 Tbs oil

1 pound pork loin cut into bitesize cubes

1 cup onions chopped

2 garlic cloves minced

5 cups chicken broth

1 (14.5 ounce) can red enchilada sauce

1 (4.5 ounce) can chopped green chile

1 tsp chili powder

1 tsp cumin

1/2 tsp oregano

1/2 tsp paprika

1/2 tsp salt

1 (30 ounce) can of hominy

DIRECTIONS

Cut up pork loin into cubes and season with 1/2 teaspoon salt. Heat oil in a large pot. Add in pork, onion and garlic. Sauté for 5 minutes. Stir in chicken broth, enchilada sauce, and green chile. Add in chili powder, cumin, oregano, and paprika. Bring to a boil. Lower heat, cover, and simmer for 40 minutes. After 40 minutes, add in hominy, then cover and simmer for 10 more minutes.

CREAMY CHICKEN AND RICE SOUP

Serves 4-6

INGREDIENTS

1 1/2 pounds chicken cut into pieces

3 carrots chopped

3 celery stalks chopped

1 onion chopped

3 garlic cloves minced

1/4 cup flour

6 cups chicken broth

1 cup half and half

1 cup long grain rice

1 Tbs olive oil

1 tsp salt

1/2 tsp pepper

1/2 tsp Italian seasoning

1/4 tsp paprika

DIRECTIONS

Cut up chicken and season with salt, pepper, Italian seasoning, and paprika. Heat up large pot or Dutch oven on the stove and add 1 Tbs olive oil. Then add in the chicken. Cook until chicken is done, or around 10 minutes. Once the chicken is done, remove from the pan and set aside. Add 1 Tbs olive oil to pan. Add in carrots, celery, and onion. Cook for 7 minutes. Add in minced garlic cloves and cook for 30 seconds. Add chicken back into pan. Pour in flour and stir for 1 minute. Pour in chicken broth and half and half and bring to a boil. Once boiling, add in rice. Lower the heat, cover and simmer for 20 minutes. Stir occasionally to prevent rice from sticking to the bottom of the pan.

27

TEXAS COWBOY STEW

Serves 5-6

This stew is delicious and perfect when you want a hearty meal on a cold day.

INGREDIENTS

1 pound ground beef

1 tsp garlic powder

1 tsp cumin

1 tsp oregano

1 tsp chili powder

1/2 tsp salt

1 onion chopped

1 pound Kielbasa sausage sliced

1 potato peeled and cubed

1 package (10 ounces) frozen mixed vegetables

1 (15 ounce) can tomato sauce

2 (15 ounce) cans Rotel

4 cups beef broth

DIRECTIONS

In large pot, brown ground beef and drain the grease. Season with garlic powder, cumin, oregano, chili powder, and salt. Add in chopped onion, Kielbasa sausage, potatoes, and frozen mixed vegetables. Pour in tomato sauce and Rotel. Add in beef broth. Bring to a boil, reduce heat, cover and simmer for 25 minutes.

CHICKEN AND DUMPLINGS

This is the easiest and most delicious version of chicken and dumplings that you will ever eat!

Serves 4

INGREDIENTS

1 can of biscuits (16.3 ounces)

32 ounces of Chicken broth

1 can Cream of Chicken (10.5 ounce)

2 cups of cooked shredded chicken

1/2 tsp pepper

DIRECTIONS

Cut up biscuits into small pieces. Pour chicken broth into a large pot and bring to a boil. Add cooked chicken into the broth. Add in Cream of chicken. Place biscuits into the pan making sure they are not stuck together. Season with 1/2 teaspoon pepper. Bring to a simmer and cook for 10 minutes while stirring occasionally.

THE BEST POTATO SOUP

This potato soup is the best you will ever eat. Its creamy and comforting and will put a smile on everyone's faces.

Serves 5-6

INGREDIENTS

7 strips of bacon chopped

4 large Russet potatoes

1 onion chopped

4 garlic cloves chopped

3 Tbs butter

1/3 cup flour

4 cups chicken broth

2 cups half and half

2/3 cup sour cream

1 1/2 tsp salt

1 tsp pepper

Shredded cheese for topping

Green onions chopped for topping

DIRECTIONS

Cook chopped bacon in a large pot and remove when crispy. Do not remove bacon grease from pot. Add in butter to pot and melt. Add chopped onion to pot and sauté for 5 minutes. Add in garlic and sauté for 1 minute. Add in the flour and stir for 1 minute. Wash and peel potatoes and chop into cubes. Add the potatoes to the pot. Pour in chicken broth and half and half. Season with salt and pepper. Bring to a boil and boil for 10 minutes until potatoes are soft and can be pierced with a fork. Place half of the soup mixture into a blender and blend. Pour the blended soup back into the pot and stir. Add in sour cream and cooked bacon. Reserve some bacon to top the bowl of soup. Simmer for 10 minutes. Top with bacon, shredded cheese, and chopped green onions.

BROCCOLI CHEESE SOUP

Serves 5-6

Broccoli cheese soup is my favorite soup of all time. I could eat this soup every day!

INGREDIENTS

1 onion chopped

1/2 stick of butter

2 gloves minced garlic

1/2 cup flour

32 ounces of chicken broth

1 cup shredded carrots

3 cups broccoli chopped

1/2 tsp salt

1 tsp garlic powder

1 tsp onion powder

1/2 tsp pepper

2 cups half and half

2 cups shredded cheddar cheese

DIRECTIONS

Melt butter in a large pot and add onion. Sauté for 5 minutes. Add garlic and cook for 1 minute. Add in salt, garlic powder, onion powder, and pepper. Add in flour and stir for 1 minute. Whisk in chicken broth. Add in carrots and broccoli. Pour in half and half. Bring to a boil, reduce heat to a simmer and cover and cook for 15 minutes. After 15 minutes, stir in shredded cheese until melted.

WHITE CHICKEN CHILI

SERVES 4-6

INGREDIENTS

1 1/2 pounds chicken cooked

1 onion chopped

1 jalapeno chopped

3 garlic cloves minced

1 Tbs olive oil

3 Tbs flour

6 cups chicken broth

2 cans Cannellini beans drained

1 Tbs Worcestershire sauce

2 (4 ounce) cans green chiles

1 can corn drained

8 ounces cream cheese

1 tsp chili powder

1/2 tsp cumin

1/2 tsp oregano

1/2 tsp salt

1/4 tsp pepper

DIRECTIONS

Pour olive oil into a large pot and heat. Add in onions and jalapeno and sauté for 5 minutes until softened. Add in minced garlic and sauté for 1 minute. Add in flour, stir and cook for 1 minute. Pour in chicken broth. Add in chili powder, cumin, oregano, salt, and pepper. Add 2 cans of green chile. Add in Worcestershire sauce. Pour in cannellini beans and corn. Add in the cooked chicken and bring to a boil. Lower heat, cover and simmer for 15-20 minutes. Remove lid and add in cream cheese. Stir until melted.

Optional: blend together 1/2 cup cannellini beans with 1/2 cup chicken broth. Poor blended beans into pot. This will make the chili creamier.

STUFFED BELL PEPPER SOUP

Serves 5-6

I love stuffed bell peppers, but I find them a little tedious to make. This stuffed bell pepper soup is the perfect solution!

INGREDIENTS

1 pound ground beef

1 onion chopped

2 bell peppers chopped

1 (28 ounce) can crushed tomatoes

4 cups beef broth

1 tsp oregano

1 tsp garlic powder

1 tsp salt

3/4 cup uncooked jasmine rice

DIRECTIONS

In a large pot, brown the ground beef and drain the grease. Once beef is cooked, add in bell peppers and onions. Cook for 5 minutes until soft. Add in oregano, garlic powder, salt, and pepper. Pour in crushed tomatoes and beef broth. Bring to a boil, lower heat, cove,r and simmer for 20 minutes. After 20 minutes, add in the uncooked jasmine rice. Cover and simmer for 20 more minutes.

THE BEST TACO SOUP

INGREDIENTS

1 pound ground beef

1 Tbs oil

1 onion chopped

2 cloves garlic

1 can (28 ounces) of crushed tomatoes

1 can (7 ounce) green chiles

1 can chili beans

1 can corn

4 cups broth

1 packet taco seasoning

1 packet ranch seasoning

1/2 tsp salt

1/2 tsp pepper

Serves 5-6

I have made several taco soup recipes and this is my favorite by far! My whole family loves it!

DIRECTIONS

Add 1 Tbs of oil into a pan. Sauté one chopped onion in oil for 2 minutes until soft. Add 1 pound ground beef to pan and cook until done. Add 2 cloves of minced garlic. Season ground beef with salt and pepper. Add 1 packet of taco seasoning and 1 packet of ranch seasoning. Add in the crushed tomatoes, chili beans, corn, and 1 can of green chiles. Pour in 4 cups of broth. Cover with lid. Bring soup to a boil, then lower temperature to low and simmer for 30 minutes.

ITALIAN WEDDING SOUP

Serves 4

INGREDIENTS

Meatballs-
1 pound ground turkey
1 egg
3/4 cup plain
breadcrumbs
2 garlic cloves minced
1/2 tsp salt
1/2 tsp pepper

1 1/2 cup carrots
chopped

1 cup celery chopped

1 small onion chopped

2 garlic cloves

1 Tbs Italian seasoning

1 1/2 tsp salt

1/2 tsp pepper

8 cups chicken broth

1/2 cup orzo pasta

6 ounces fresh spinach

DIRECTIONS

For the meatballs:
Combine ground turkey, egg,
breadcrumbs, garlic, salt, and
pepper. Form into 20 meatballs.
Bake at 400 degrees for 20
minutes.

In a pan, heat 1 Tbs oil and add
carrots, celery, and onion. Sauté
for 5 minutes. Add in garlic and
sauté for 1 minute. Season with
Italian seasoning, salt, and
pepper. Pour in chicken broth
and bring to a boil. Add in
meatballs and orzo. Simmer for
10 minutes. Stir in spinach.

Main DISHES

MONTEREY CHICKEN SPAGHETTI

Serves 6-8

This is a wonderful twist on classic chicken spaghetti. The fried onions and spinach take this recipe to another level!

INGREDIENTS

12 ounces spaghetti pasta

4 cups cooked chicken cubed

16 ounces sour cream

2 cans cream of chicken soup

10 ounces frozen spinach, thawed and drained

2 cups Monterey Jack cheese shredded

2 garlic cloves minced

6 ounces of French fried onions

DIRECTIONS

Preheat oven to 350 degrees. Cook spaghetti as directed on package, drain, and set aside. In a large bowl, combine chicken, cream of chicken soup, sour cream, spinach, garlic, 1 cup of Monterey jack cheese, and 1/2 of the can of French fried onions. Stir in the cooked spaghetti. Pour mixture into either a 9X13 inch pan or 2 9X9 inch pans. Top with the remaining 1 cup of Monterey Jack cheese and the rest of the French fried onions. Bake uncovered for 40-50 minutes.

Easy
CHEESEBURGER SLIDERS

SERVES **4-5**

INGREDIENTS

2 pounds of ground beef

1/2 cup breadcrumbs

3/4 cup chopped onions

1 clove minced garlic

1/2 tsp salt

1/2 tsp pepper

6 slices of cheese

1 package of slider buns

DIRECTIONS

Preheat oven to 400 degrees. In a bowl, mix together ground beef, breadcrumbs, onions, garlic, salt, and pepper. Spread mixture out on a 9X13 inch pan and press into the shape of a rectangle. Bake for 25 minutes. Remove from oven and place cheese slices on top of meat. Bake for 2 more minutes until cheese is melted. Cut meat into squares and place on slider buns.

BEEF STROGANOFF

SERVES 5-6

INGREDIENTS

2 pounds sirloin steak cut into strips

1/4 cup flour

1 Tbs olive oil

1 onion chopped

8 ounces sliced mushrooms

2 garlic cloves minced

1/4 cup butter

3 cups beef broth

2 Tbs Worcestershire sauce

1 cup sour cream

1 Tbs Dijon mustard

salt and pepper to taste

1 pound egg noodles

DIRECTIONS

Cook the egg noodles as directed on package, drain and set aside. Slice sirloin steak into thin strips cutting against the grain. Season with salt and pepper. Sprinkle the flour on the steak coating all of the steak. Heat oil in pan and add onion and mushrooms. Sauté for 7 minutes. Add garlic and sauté for 30 seconds. Remove from skillet and set aside. Add butter to skillet and melt. Add steak and cook until browned. Return onion and mushrooms to the pan. Pour in beef broth and Worcestershire sauce. Bring to a boil and simmer for 2-3 minutes until liquid thickens up. Add in sour cream and Dijon mustard and stir. Add salt and pepper to taste. Serve over egg noodles.

TACO PIZZA

SERVES 3-4

I love pizza and I love tacos! If you put them together you will have the most delicious taco pizza that the whole family will love.

INGREDIENTS

1 can Pillsbury Pizza Crust

1 pound ground beef

1 packet taco seasoning

1 can refried beans

2 cups shredded cheese

Shredded lettuce for topping

Tomatoes for topping

DIRECTIONS

Place pizza crust on 9X13 inch pan. Bake at 400 degrees for 8 minutes. Remove from oven. Spread a layer of refried beans over the crust. Brown the ground beef and add it on top of the beans. Sprinkle shredded cheese on the ground beef. Place back in oven and bake 10 more minutes or until crust is done. Remove from oven and top with shredded lettuce and tomatoes.

SPICY SALMON WITH AVOCADO AND CUCUMBER SALAD

SERVES 2

INGREDIENTS

2 salmon filets

1 tsp olive oil

1/2 tsp salt

1/2 tsp garlic powder

1/4 tsp paprika

1/8 tsp pepper

1/2 avocado chopped

1/2 cucumber chopped

1/2 lime

1/4 cup mayo

1 Tbs soy sauce

1 tsp Sriracha

DIRECTIONS

Preheat oven to 450 degrees. Drizzle olive oil on salmon. Season the salmon filets with salt, pepper, garlic powder, and paprika. Bake for 12-15 minutes.

Cucumber and avocado Salad: Chop the avocado and cucumber and season with a dash of salt. Squeeze the juice of 1/2 lime on top.

Spicy Mayo: Mix 1/4 cup of mayo with 1 Tbs of soy sauce and 1 tsp of sriracha.

Top the salmon filet with the cucumber and avocado salad. Then drizzle spicy mayo on top.

CHIPOTLE CHICKEN BURGER WITH AVOCADO

SERVES 6

This burger is juicy, spicy, and delicious. This is a great option to kick up your regular burger night.

INGREDIENTS

2 pounds ground chicken

1/2 onion chopped

1 garlic cloves minced

1 tsp salt

½ tsp pepper

6 hamburger buns

Avocado

For Chipotle Mayo:

½ cup mayo

1 can chipotle peppers in Adobo sauce

1 Tablespoon of Adobo sauce from can

Juice of 1 lime

DIRECTIONS

Mix together ground chicken, onion, garlic, salt, and pepper. Form into 6 patties. Cook patties either on grill or in skillet until internal temperature reaches 165 degrees.

For Chipotle Mayo:
Blend together mayo, 1 chipotle pepper, 1 tablespoon of the chipotle sauce, and the juice of 1 lime.

Toast your hamburger buns, then add your patties to buns. Top with the Chipotle mayo and sliced avocado.

EASY BAKED CHEESE TORTELLINI

SERVES 5-6

This is a quick and easy way to make a hearty dish that makes it seem like you spent hours in the kitchen.

INGREDIENTS

1 pound ground beef

1/2 onion chopped

2-3 garlic cloves minced

2 tsp Italian seasoning

24 ounce jar of Marinara sauce

18-20 ounces tortellini

2 cups shredded mozzarella cheese

1/2 tsp salt

1/2 tsp pepper

DIRECTIONS

Preheat oven to 375 degrees. Cook ground beef in pan until almost done. Then add in the chopped onion and cook until meat is done and onion is soft. Drain the grease. Add in minced garlic and cook for 1 minute. Add in Italian seasoning, salt, and pepper. Pour in jar of marinara sauce and uncooked tortellini. Add in 1 cup of shredded mozzarella and stir. Pour into a 9X13 inch pan. Top with remaining mozzarella cheese. Bake for 30 minutes.

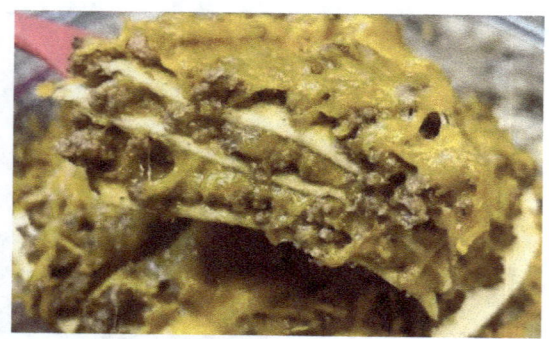

TACO BAKE

SERVES **4**

INGREDIENTS

1 pound ground beef

1 packet of taco seasoning

1/2 cup Salsa Con Queso

3 flour tortillas

2 cups shredded cheese

DIRECTIONS

Preheat oven to 350 degrees. Brown 1 pound of ground beef and drain the grease. Add in 1 packet of taco seasoning. Add the Salsa Con Queso and stir until combined. Spray a round pan with cooking spray. Add one tortilla in the bottom of the pan. Spread 1/3 of meat mixture onto tortilla. Add 1/3 of the shredded cheese on top of meat mixture. Repeat two more times until there are 3 layers. Bake for 15 to 20 minutes.

Homemade Hamburger Helper

SERVES 4-5

INGREDIENTS

1 pound ground beef

1 yellow onion chopped

2 garlic cloves minced

2 Tbs flour

3 cups beef broth

1- 8 ounce can of tomato sauce

8 ounces pasta shells

1/2 cup heavy cream or half and half

2 cups cheddar cheese shredded

1 Tbs olive oil

1/2 tsp Italian seasoning

1 tsp salt

1/2 tsp garlic powder

DIRECTIONS

Cook ground beef and drain the grease. Remove from pan and set aside. Add 1 tablespoon of oil to a pan and add chopped onion. Sauté for 5 minutes. Add minced garlic and cook for 30 seconds. Add flour and stir cooking for 1 minute. Pour in beef broth and tomato sauce. Add in Italian seasoning, salt, garlic powder, and onion powder. Bring to a boil. Add in pasta shells and bring to boil. Lower temp to a simmer, cover and cook for 12-15 minutes until pasta shells are done. Pour in the heavy cream and add in the shredded cheese. Stir until cheese is melted. Add in the cooked ground beef and stir.

ZUCCHINI, BEEF, RICE AND CHEESE SKILLET

SERVES 4

Who doesn't love a one pot meal? This is an easy dish you can throw together quickly that everyone will rave about.

INGREDIENTS

1 pound ground beef

½ onion chopped

8 ounces of sliced mushrooms

2 garlic cloves minced

2 zucchinis chopped

1 packet of onion soup mix

1 cup of uncooked rice

1 1/2 cup chicken broth

1 cup shredded cheese

DIRECTIONS

Brown ground beef in a large pan. Add in onion, mushrooms, garlic and zucchini. Cook for 5 minutes until vegetables are soft. Add in onions soup mix, uncooked rice, and chicken broth. Cover and simmer for 15 minutes. Top with cheese and serve.

EASY PICADILLO

SERVES 4-5

INGREDIENTS

1 pound ground beef

1 bell pepper chopped

1/2 onion chopped

2 small potatoes or 1 large potato diced into cubes

2 garlic cloves minced

8 ounces tomato sauce

2 cups beef broth

1 tsp cumin

1 tsp salt

1/2 tsp pepper

1 bay leaf

DIRECTIONS

Cook the ground beef in a pan until done. Add in the cumin, salt, pepper and garlic. Cook for 1 minute. Add in the bell pepper and onion and cook for 1-2 minutes. Add in potatoes. Pour in tomato sauce and beef broth. Add in Bay leaf. Bring to a boil then reduce heat and cover and simmer for 20 minutes.

KING RANCH CASSEROLE

SERVES 5-6

INGREDIENTS

3 cups cooked chicken

1 bell pepper chopped

1 onion chopped

1 Tbs olive oil

1 can cream of
mushroom soup

1 can cream of chicken
soup

1 can of Rotel

1/2 tsp salt

1/2 tsp pepper

2 cups shredded
cheese

12 corn tortillas

DIRECTIONS

Preheat oven to 375 degrees. Sauté bell
pepper and onion in olive oil for 5 minutes
and remove. In a bowl, mix together the
bell pepper, onion, cooked chicken, cream
of mushroom soup, cream of chicken soup,
Rotel, salt, and pepper. In a 9X13 inch pan,
place 6 corn tortillas covering the bottom
of the pan. Pour ½ of the chicken mixture
on top of tortillas and cover with 1 cup
shredded cheese. Repeat by placing 6
more corn tortillas on top of cheese. Then
pour the remaining chicken mixture on top
of tortillas and covering with 1 cup
shredded cheese. Bake for 30 minutes.

BEEF TIPS

SERVES 4-5

INGREDIENTS

2-3 pounds top sirloin

1 onion chopped

1 Tbs vegetable oil

1 Tbs beef bullion

2 Tbs Worcestershire sauce

2 cups water

1 packet brown gravy mix

1 tsp garlic powder

1/2 tsp pepper

DIRECTIONS

To a pan, add 1 Tbs of vegetable oil. Add in one chopped onion and sauté on medium low for 5 minutes until softened. Remove from pan. Cut top sirloin into cubes. Season meat with garlic powder and pepper. Add sirloin to the pan and cook on all sides for 2-3 minutes until browned. Add 1 Tbs of beef bouillon and 2 Tbs of Worcestershire sauce to meat in pan. Add the cooked onions back into the pan. Pour in 2 cups of water. Add in 1 packet of brown gravy mix to pan. Bring to a boil then lower temp and cover pan. Simmer on low for 50 minutes.

MUSHROOM AND SPINACH PASTA

SERVES 4-5

This is a wonderfully easy meatless meal that comes together quickly.

INGREDIENTS

1 ounces pasta (farfalle)

2 Tbs olive oil

2-3 garlic cloves minced

16 ounces mushrooms

10 ounces fresh spinach

1/2 cup vegetable or chicken broth

1 tsp Italian seasoning

1/2 tsp salt

1/2 tsp pepper

1/2 cup parmesan cheese

DIRECTIONS

Boil pasta as directed on package. Drain and set aside. In a pan, add olive oil and heat over medium. Add mushrooms and sauté for 4-5 minutes. Add garlic and cook 1 minute. Pour in chicken broth. Add spinach to pan and cook 2-3 minutes until spinach is wilted. Season with salt, pepper, and Italian seasoning. Add cooked pasta into the pan and mix. Stir in parmesan cheese.

BAKED CHICKEN AND RICE

SERVES 5-6

INGREDIENTS

6 boneless chicken thighs

5 strips of bacon chopped

1 onion chopped

3 gloves minced garlic

1 1/2 cups jasmine rice

4 cups chicken broth

1/2 tsp salt

1/2 tsp garlic powder

1/2 tsp smoked paprika

1/4 tsp pepper

DIRECTIONS

Preheat oven to 400 degrees. Cook bacon in a pan and remove from the pan leaving the bacon grease. Sauté the onion in the pan with bacon grease for 5 minutes. Add in garlic and cook for 1 minute. In the bottom of a 9X13 inch pan, add uncooked jasmine rice, sautéed onions, garlic, and bacon. Pour in chicken broth and stir. Season chicken thighs with salt, garlic powder, smoked paprika, and pepper. Place chicken thighs into the 9x13 inch pan. Cover with foil and bake for 45 minutes. Remove foil and bake an additional 15 minutes.

MINI BBQ CHEDDAR MEATLOAF

SERVES 4-5

This isn't your moms traditional meatloaf. This meatloaf is flavored with melty cheese and sweet and tangy BBQ sauce.

INGREDIENTS

2 pounds ground beef

1/2 cup panko breadcrumbs

1 tsp garlic powder

1 tsp onion powder

1 tsp salt

1 Tbs Worcestershire sauce

1 tsp mustard

1/4 cup barbeque sauce of choice

1 cup shredded cheese

2 eggs

DIRECTIONS

Preheat oven to 425 degrees. Mix together ground beef, panko breadcrumbs, garlic powder, onion powder, salt, Worcestershire sauce, mustard, barbeque sauce, shredded cheese, and eggs. Form into small circular loafs (10-12) and place on baking sheet. Brush the top of the loaf with barbeque sauce. Bake for 25 minutes.

GREEN CHILE CASSEROLE

SERVES 4-5

INGREDIENTS

1 pound ground beef

1 can cream of mushroom soup

1 (4 ounce) can green chiles

1 bag tortilla chips

2 cups shredded cheese

1/2 tsp salt

1/2 tsp pepper

DIRECTIONS

Preheat oven to 350 degrees. Brown ground beef in pan and season with salt and pepper. Drain the grease from pan. Add in cream of mushroom soup and green chiles. In a 9x13 inch pan, place a layer of tortilla chips to cover the bottom of the pan. Add half of the meat mixture on top of the tortilla chips. Cover meat mixture with 1 cup cheese. Repeat these steps and place another layer of chips. Add the remaining meat mixture and cover with 1 cup cheese. Bake for 25 minutes.

ROASTED BROCCOLI AND RICOTTA PASTA

SERVES 4-5

INGREDIENTS

12 ounces pasta

1 head of broccoli chopped

2 Tbs olive oil

16 ounces Ricotta cheese

3 cloves garlic

1/2 lemon

1/2 tsp salt

1/4 tsp pepper

3/4 cup of reserved pasta water

DIRECTIONS

Preheat oven to 400 degrees. Place broccoli on a baking sheet and drizzle with 1 Tbs olive oil. Season with salt and pepper. Bake for 20 minutes. Boil pasta as directed on package and drain. In a pan, heat 1 Tbs olive oil and sauté 3 cloves of garlic. Squeeze in the juice of half of a lemon. Stir in the Ricotta cheese until melted and season with salt and pepper. Pour in the reserved pasta water and stir. Add in the cooked pasta and roasted broccoli.

SLOPPY JOES

SERVES 4-5

INGREDIENTS

2 pounds ground beef

1 onion chopped

1 bell pepper chopped

2 Tbs tomato paste

1/2 cup ketchup

2 garlic cloves minced

1 cup water

2 Tbs brown sugar

2 Tbs Worcestershire sauce

2 Tbs mustard

1/2 tsp salt

1/2 tsp pepper

Hamburger buns

DIRECTIONS

Brown ground beef, then add in onions and bell peppers. Cook for 5 minutes. Add in tomato paste, ketchup, garlic, and water. Add brown sugar, Worcestershire sauce, mustard, salt and pepper. Cover and simmer for 10 minutes.
Serve on a toasted bun.

SAUCY MEATBALLS

SERVES 5-6

If you have never made homemade meatballs, this is the recipe that you need to try. These are easy and the most delicious meatballs I have ever had.

INGREDIENTS

1 1/2 pounds ground beef

3 cloves garlic minced

1 cup plain breadcrumbs

1 cup shredded parmesan cheese

2 eggs

1 tsp salt

24 ounce jar of marinara sauce

2 cups shredded mozzarella cheese

DIRECTIONS

Preheat oven to 400 degrees. Mix together ground beef, garlic, breadcrumbs, parmesan cheese, eggs, and salt. Form into 1-inch meatballs. This makes around 24 meatballs. Place meatballs on a greased baking sheet and bake for 20 minutes. Once meatballs are done, place them in a 9x13 inch baking dish. Cover meatballs with marinara sauce. Top with mozzarella cheese. Cover with foil and bake for 20 minutes. Remove foil and bake an additional 10 minutes.

Tip:
These meatballs freeze wonderfully. Bake half of them now and freeze the other half for an easy meal later.

CHEESEBURGER PASTA

SERVES 4-5

INGREDIENTS

16 ounces elbow pasta

1 pound ground beef

1/2 onion chopped

1/2 tsp salt

1/2 tsp onion powder

1/2 tsp garlic powder

1/4 tsp pepper

8 ounces cream cheese

8 ounces shredded
cheddar cheese

1 cup milk

DIRECTIONS

Boil pasta as directed on package, drain, and set aside. In a pan, cook ground beef and drain the grease. Add in onion and season with salt, onion powder, garlic powder, and pepper. Add in cream cheese and shredded cheddar cheese and stir until melted. Pour in milk and stir. Mix in the cooked pasta.

CHEESY SAUSAGE, RICE AND BROCCOLI SKILLET

SERVES 4-5

This is a one pan meal that is easy and so beautiful. Your family will love you for making this!

INGREDIENTS

14 ounces of Kielbasa sausage cut into slices

1 onion chopped

1 bell pepper chopped

2 garlic cloves minced

1/2 tsp salt

1/2 tsp pepper

1 cup rice uncooked (not instant rice)

2 cups chicken broth

2 cups raw broccoli chopped into bite size pieces

2 cups shredded cheddar cheese

DIRECTIONS

In a large skillet, brown the Kielbasa sausage on both sides then remove from pan. Sauté onion and bell pepper for around 5 minutes until soft. Add garlic, salt, and pepper. Cook for 1 minute. Add rice to pan and stir. Pour in chicken broth and bring to a boil. Lower heat to a simmer, cover, and cook for 15 minutes. After 15 minutes, add in the broccoli on top of the rice. Do not stir in the broccoli in yet. Cover and cook for 7 minutes. After 7 minutes, uncover pan and add in Kielbasa sausage and 1 cup of the shredded cheese. Mix together. Top with remaining cup of shredded cheese. Cover for 1-2 more minutes until cheese is melted.

Hidden Veggie Pasta

SERVES 4-5

This is a great way to pack in veggies without anyone noticing. If you have a picky eater in the house, then this recipe is for you!

INGREDIENTS

1 carrot chopped

1 bell pepper sliced

10 ounces cherry tomatoes

1/2 onion chopped

1 zucchini sliced

3-4 garlic cloves

1 Tbs olive oil

2 Tbs tomato paste

2 cups chicken broth

1 teaspoon Italian seasoning

Salt and pepper to taste

16 ounces pasta

DIRECTIONS

Cook pasta as directed on package and set aside.
Heat olive oil in a large pan and add in carrot, bell pepper, cherry tomatoes, onion, zucchini and garlic cloves. Sauté for 7-8 minutes until vegetables are soft. Add in tomato paste and chicken broth. Season with Italian seasoning, salt, and pepper. Cover and simmer for 10 minutes. Transfer to a blender and blend until smooth. Pour back into the pan. Add in the pasta and toss in the sauce.

THAI CHICKEN LETTUCE WRAPS

SERVES 4-5

This is a healthy and delicious meal that is great for when you're wanting takeout but don't want to spend extra on the takeout prices!

INGREDIENTS

2 tsp sesame oil

1/2 cup chopped onion

4 cloves garlic minced

1 tsp ginger minced

2 pounds ground chicken

1/3 cup soy sauce

1/3 cup sweet chili sauce

1/2 cup chopped cashews

1 bunch green onion chopped

1 cup shredded carrots

Salt and pepper to taste

Butter Lettuce leaves

DIRECTIONS

Add sesame oil to a large pan and heat. Add in onions and sauté for 2-3 minutes. Add in garlic and ginger and cook for 2 minutes. Add ground chicken and season and salt and pepper. Cook until chicken is done. Pour in soy sauce and sweet chili sauce. Mix until combined. Sprinkle in chopped cashews, green onion, and carrots. Remove from stove. Serve the chicken in the butter lettuce leaves.

CROCKPOT
MEALS

CROCKPOT TACO HASHBROWN CASSEROLE

SERVES 5-6

INGREDIENTS

1 pound ground beef

2 garlic cloves minced

1 packet of taco seasoning

1 can (10.5 ounce) cream of chicken soup

30 ounces frozen shredded hash-browns

2 cups shredded cheese

1/2 tsp salt

1/2 tsp pepper

DIRECTIONS

Brown the ground beef until done and add in garlic and salt and pepper. Pour the ground beef in large bowl. Add in the taco seasoning, cream of chicken soup, hash-browns, and 1 cup of the shredded cheese. Stir until combined. Place mixture into a greased crockpot. Cover with the remaining cup of shredded cheese. Cover and cook on low for 4 hours or high for 2-3 hours.

CROCKPOT CARNE GUISADA

SERVES 5-6

INGREDIENTS

2-3 pounds chuck steak

1 onion chopped

1 bell pepper chopped

3 garlic cloves minced

1 jalapeno chopped

2 cups beef broth

1 (15 ounce) can diced tomatoes

2 Tbs oil

1 tsp cumin

1 tsp chili powder

1 tsp oregano

6 Tbs flour

Salt and pepper to taste

DIRECTIONS

Cut the chuck steak into cubes and season with salt and pepper. Add 1 Tbs of oil into a pan and add the steak. Cook on all sides around 2-3 minutes until browned. Remove steak from pan and put into crockpot. Add 1 Tbs of oil to a pan. Add onion, bell pepper, and garlic. Sauté for 2-3 minutes. Add in cumin, chili powder, oregano, and flour. Cook for 5 minutes stirring until flour is absorbed. Add the cooked vegetables into the crockpot. Add in the chopped jalapeno. Pour in the beef broth and the diced tomatoes into the crockpot. Cover and cook on high for 4 hours or low 6-8 hours.

CROCKPOT BUFFALO CHICKEN MEATBALLS

SERVES 4-5

INGREDIENTS

2 pounds ground chicken

1 cup Panko bread crumbs

2 eggs

1 cup parmesan cheese

1 tsp garlic powder

1 tsp onion powder

1/2 teaspoon salt

1/4 tsp pepper

1 1/2 cups buffalo Sauce

1/4 cup ranch dressing

DIRECTIONS

Mix together ground chicken, panko bread crumbs, eggs, parmesan cheese, garlic powder, onion powder, paprika, salt and pepper. Form into meatballs and place on a 9X13 inch pan. Bake meatballs at 400 degrees for 12 minutes. Pour buffalo sauce and ranch dressing into the crockpot. Add in cooked meatballs. Cover and cook on high for 2 hours.

CROCKPOT CHICKEN SPAGHETTI

SERVES 5-6

INGREDIENTS

1 pound chicken breast

1 can cream of mushroom soup

1 can cream of chicken soup

1 can Rotel

4 ounces of cream cheese

1 tsp garlic powder

1 Tbs Italian seasoning

12 ounces of spaghetti pasta

2 cups shredded cheese

DIRECTIONS

Into a Crockpot, add the cream of mushroom soup, cream of chicken soup, Rotel, and cream cheese. Place chicken on top of mixture. Season chicken with garlic powder and Italian seasoning. Cook on low for 4-6 hours until chicken is done. Once chicken is done, remove from Crockpot and shred. Put shredded chicken back into crockpot mixture and stir. Boil 12 ounces of spaghetti pasta until done and drain. Add the pasta into the crockpot mixture and stir. Add in 2 cups of shredded cheese and stir until cheese is melted.

CROCKPOT BEEF AND BROCCOLI

SERVES 4-5

INGREDIENTS

2-3 pounds beef chuck roast

1 cup beef broth

1/2 cup soy sauce

1/3 cup dark brown sugar

1 Tbs sesame oil

3 garlic cloves minced

1/2 cup cornstarch

14 ounce bag frozen broccoli

DIRECTIONS

Slice beef chuck roast into small strips and place in the crockpot. In a bowl, mix together beef broth, soy sauce, dark brown sugar, sesame oil, and garlic. Pour over the beef. Cook on high for 4 hours or low for 6 hours. 1 hour before it is done, mix together 1/4 cup of cornstarch with 1/4 cup of the liquid from crockpot. Pour back into crockpot. 30 minutes before you are ready to eat, add in the frozen broccoli and cover.

CROCKPOT CARNITAS

SERVES 5-6

INGREDIENTS

4 pounds pork butt or shoulder

1 onion chopped

4 garlic cloves minced

1 orange

2 limes

1 Tbs oregano

2 tsp cumin

1 tsp chili powder

2 tsp salt

1 tsp pepper

DIRECTIONS

Rub the seasonings all over the pork butt or shoulder. Place in a crockpot. Squeeze the juice of 1 orange and 2 limes into the crockpot. Add the chopped onions and garlic to the crockpot. Cover and cook on low for 8-10 hours or high for 5-6 hours. Shred the meat once it is done. Serve in a taco shell topped with your favorite toppings.

BBQ CHICKEN STUFFED BAKED POTATOES

SERVES 4

This entire meal is made in the Crockpot. This is an easy no mess meal that everyone will love.

INGREDIENTS

2 pounds boneless skinless chicken breast

1 Tbs barbeque seasoning

1 bottle BBQ sauce- 18 oz

4 small potatoes or 2 large potatoes

DIRECTIONS

Wash and dry potatoes and wrap in foil. Place a large piece of foil inside half of the crockpot to make a divider. Place the wrapped potatoes inside of the foil divider in the crockpot. Season the chicken breast with the BBQ seasoning of choice. Pour 1 cup of BBQ sauce in the bottom of the other half of the crockpot. Place chicken on top of BBQ sauce. Pour the rest of the BBQ sauce on top of chicken. Cover and cook on low for 7-8 hours or on high for 5-6 hours. Remove potatoes from crockpot along with foil divider. Shred the chicken in the crockpot and stir. Serve the BBQ chicken on top of the potato.

CROCKPOT BOURBON CHICKEN

SERVES 4-5

INGREDIENTS

2 pounds chicken breast or chicken thighs

Salt and pepper to taste

1/4 cup bourbon (may also substitute with chicken broth)

3/4 cup brown sugar

1/3 cup soy sauce

2 cloves of minced garlic

2 Tbs water

3 Tbs cornstarch

DIRECTIONS

Placed chicken into the Crockpot. Season the chicken with salt and pepper. Add in the bourbon, brown sugar, soy sauce, and minced garlic. Cover and cook on low for 6 hours or high for 4 hours. 30 minutes before its done, mix together water and cornstarch. Pour into the crock pot and stir. Cover and cook for the remaining 30 minutes. Once it's done, break up chicken into smaller pieces and serve.

CROCKPOT BEEF RAMEN

SERVES 4

INGREDIENTS

1 pound ground beef

2 cloves minced garlic

1 cup shredded cabbage

1 bell pepper cut into strips

1 bunch green onions chopped

1/4 cup soy sauce

1 Tbs brown sugar

14 ounces beef broth 2 packs ramen noodles (remove flavor packet)

2 cups water

DIRECTIONS

Brown the ground beef in a pan and drain the grease. Add in the minced garlic and cook for 1 minute. Add the ground beef into the crockpot. To the crockpot, add in shredded cabbage, bell pepper, green onions, soy sauce, brown sugar, beef broth and water. Cover and cook on low for 4 hours or high for 2 hours. 30 minutes before you are ready to eat, add in 2 packets of ramen noodles. You will not add the flavor packet. Once noodled are cooked, stir and enjoy.

CROCKPOT ORANGE TERIYAKI MEATBALLS

SERVES 4-5

INGREDIENTS

20-25 meatballs, frozen or homemade

1/2 cup orange marmalade

1/2 cup teriyaki sauce

1 cup barbeque sauce

1 tsp garlic powder

1 tsp pepper

DIRECTIONS

To the crockpot, add in meatballs, orange marmalade, teriyaki sauce, barbeque sauce, garlic powder, and pepper. Cook on low for 4 hours

CROCKPOT SWEDISH MEATBALLS

SERVES 4-5

INGREDIENTS

1 (30 ounce) bag frozen meatballs

1 can cream of mushroom soup

1 can beef broth

1 cup water

1 packet brown gravy mix

2 tsp garlic powder

1 cup sour cream

Egg noodles to serve over

DIRECTIONS

In a bowl, mix together cream of mushroom soup, beef broth, water, brown gravy mix, and garlic powder. Pour mixture into the crockpot. Add in the bag of frozen meatballs. Cook on low for 4 hours. Once you are ready to eat, mix in 1 cup of sour cream. Serve over egg noodles.

CROCKPOT FRENCH DIP SANDWICHES

SERVES 4-5

INGREDIENTS

2-3 pound chuck roast

1 onion sliced

1 packet Au Jus Gravy mix

2 cans French onion soup

2 cups water

1/2 tsp salt

1/2 tsp pepper

6 slices provolone cheese

Hoagie rolls

DIRECTIONS

Place chuck roast in crockpot and season with salt and pepper. Add in onion, Au Jus Gravy mix, French onion soup, and water. Cook on low for 7-8 hours. Once done, shred meat. Place meat on the hoagie roll and top with provolone cheese. Bake sandwiches in oven at 350 for 2-3 minutes until cheese is melted. Serve with a bowl of juice from crockpot to dip the sandwich in.

CROCKPOT HONEY GARLIC CHICKEN

SERVES 4-5

INGREDIENTS

2 pounds chicken
(breast or thighs)

1/3 cup soy sauce

1/3 cup ketchup

1/3 cup honey

3-4 garlic cloves
minced

1 tsp sesame seeds

2 Tbs cornstarch

2 Tbs water

DIRECTIONS

Place chicken in bottom of crockpot. In a bowl, mix the soy sauce, ketchup, honey, and garlic. Pour mixture over chicken. Cover and cook on low for 5-6 hours or high for 3-4 hours. 30 minutes before you are going to eat, mix the cornstarch and water and pour into crockpot. Cover back up for 30 minutes. Top with sesame seeds when done.

CROCKPOT SALSA VERDE CHICKEN

SERVES 4-5

INGREDIENTS

2 pounds chicken breast

1 (16 ounce) jar of Salsa Verde

1 small onion sliced

1 tsp garlic powder

1/2 tsp cumin

1/2 tsp salt

1/2 tsp pepper

DIRECTIONS

Add all of the ingredients into the crockpot. Cover and cook on high for 5-6 hours or on low for 7-8 hours. Shred the chicken when done.

CROCKPOT NASHVILLE HOT CHICKEN SLIDERS

SERVES 4-5

INGREDIENTS

2 pounds chicken breast

1 Tbs brown sugar

1 tsp garlic powder

1 tsp onion powder

1 tsp paprika

1/2 tsp salt

2 Tbs butter

Sauce
4 Tbs butter melted

2 Tbs brown sugar

1/2 to 1 tsp cayenne pepper

1/2 tsp garlic powder

1/2 tsp onion powder

1/2 tsp salt

DIRECTIONS

Place chicken into crockpot. Season with brown sugar, garlic powder, onion powder, paprika, and salt. Mix until chicken is coated. Place 2 Tbs of sliced butter on top of chicken. Cover and cook on low for 5-6 hours or high for 3-4 hours. Once chicken is done, shred.

For the sauce: Melt 4 Tbs butter in a pan. Stir in cayenne pepper, garlic powder, onion powder, salt, and brown sugar. Pour sauce into the chicken and mix.

Serve on slider buns. Top with ranch dressing and pickles.

SIDE DISHES

JALAPENO CHEDDAR CORNBREAD

INGREDIENTS

1 1/2 cup cornmeal

1 cup flour

1/4 cup sugar

4 tsp baking powder

1 tsp salt

2 cups buttermilk

1 egg

1 cup shredded
cheddar cheese

4 jalapenos chopped

6 Tbs melted butter

DIRECTIONS

Preheat oven to 425 degrees. Mix
together cornmeal, flour, sugar,
baking soda, and salt. In a separate
bowl, mix together buttermilk, 3 Tbs
melted butter, and egg. Pour wet
ingredients into dry ingredients and
mix until smooth. Stir in shredded
cheese and jalapenos. Melt butter
into a 12 inch cast iron skillet or
baking dish. Pour in cornbread
mixture and bake for 25 to 30
minutes.

PARMESAN SPINACH ORZO

INGREDIENTS

1 onion chopped

1 Tbs olive oil

2 garlic cloves minced

1 Tablespoon olive oil

1 cup orzo

1/2 tsp salt

1/4 tsp pepper

2 cups chicken broth

2 cups fresh spinach

3/4 cup shredded parmesan cheese

DIRECTIONS

Add olive oil to a pan over medium heat. Add onion to pan and sauté for 5 minutes until soft. Season with salt and pepper. Add in minced garlic and cook for 1 minute. To the pan, add in orzo and the chicken broth and stir. Add in the spinach, cover and cook for 8 minutes. Sprinkle in parmesan cheese and stir.

EASY BAKED BEANS

INGREDIENTS

1 can of baked beans (55 ounces)

1 pound ground beef

1 chopped onion

1 cup BBQ sauce

2 Tbs mustard

1/4 cup brown sugar

1/2 tsp garlic powder

1/2 tsp onion powder

1/2 tsp salt

1/2 tsp pepper

DIRECTIONS

Preheat oven to 350 degrees. Cook the ground beef in a pan until done and add onion. Sauté for 5 minutes until onion is soft. Drain the grease if needed. Season the meat mixture with garlic powder, onion powder, salt, and pepper. In a large bowl, pour in the baked beans and the meat mixture. Add in brown sugar, mustard, and BBQ sauce. Stir until combined. Pour into a 9X13 pan. Bake for 45 minutes to 1 hour.

BAKED BROCCOLI
AND CHEESE CUPS
Yields 12

INGREDIENTS

2 (10 ounce) packages
frozen broccoli

15 Ritz crackers

1/2 tsp salt

1/2 tsp garlic powder

1/4 tsp pepper

1 cup shredded
cheese

1 egg

DIRECTIONS

Preheat oven to 375 degrees.
Cook frozen broccoli as
directed on package. Crush up
the Ritz crackers. In a bowl, mix
together the broccoli, Ritz
crackers, salt, pepper, garlic
powder, shredded cheese, and
egg. Place broccoli mixture into
the cups of a greased muffin
pan. Bake for 15 minutes.

CAPRESE PASTA SALAD

INGREDIENTS

8 ounces cavatappi pasta

12 ounces cherry tomatoes

1/4 cup basil chopped

8 ounces fresh mozzarella cheese

1/2 tsp salt

1/2 tsp pepper

1 (16 ounce) bottle Italian dressing

DIRECTIONS

Boil pasta as directed on package. Drain and rinse under cold water. Set aside. Cut cherry tomatoes in half and mozzarella cheese in bite size pieces. Mix together cooked pasta, tomatoes, mozzarella cheese, basil, salt and pepper. Pour Italian dressing over pasta. Refrigerate for at least 1 hour before eating.

CHEESY SCALLOPED POTATOES

INGREDIENTS

2 large potatoes peeled and sliced thin

1/2 onion chopped

1 garlic clove minced

1 1/2 cup milk

2 cups shredded cheese

1 Tbs butter

1 Tbs olive oil

2 Tbs flour

1/4 tsp salt

1/4 tsp pepper

1/4 tsp ground mustard

1/4 tsp paprika

DIRECTIONS

Preheat oven to 400 degrees. Add the butter and olive oil into a pan and then add the chopped onion. Sauté for 5 minutes. Add the garlic clove and cook for 1 minute. Add the flour into the pan with the onions and cook for 1 minute. Gradually add the milk while whisking. Add in the seasonings and stir. Take the pan off of the heat and add in 1 cup of the shredded cheese. Stir until combined. Place half of the potatoes in the bottom of a 9X13 inch pan. Pour half of the cheese sauce over the potatoes. Add the rest of the potatoes to the pan and pour the remaining cheese sauce on top. Top with 1 cup of shredded cheese. Bake for 1 hour.

CRISPY PARMESAN SWEET POTATO FRIES

INGREDIENTS

2 large sweet potatoes

2 Tbs olive oil

1 tsp salt

1 tsp garlic powder

1 tsp smoked paprika

1 tsp dried parsley

1/2 tsp pepper

1/4 cup shredded parmesan cheese

DIRECTIONS

Preheat oven to 400 degrees. Peel and cut sweet potatoes into 1/4 inch strips. In a bowl, pour olive oil over sweet potatoes and mix until coated. Season with salt, garlic powder, smoked paprika, dried parsley, and pepper. Add in shredded parmesan cheese and mix. Bake for 30 minutes. Then broil on high for 2-3 minutes.

ZUCCHINI AND TOMATO PIE

INGREDIENTS

2 zucchinis sliced

1 large tomato sliced

8 ounces whipped cream cheese

1 Tbs milk

1 garlic clove minced

1 cup Italian cheese blend

1/2 tsp salt

1/2 tsp pepper

DIRECTIONS

Preheat oven to 400 degrees. Slice zucchini and tomato into 1/4 inch thick slices. Season with salt and pepper. In a bowl, mix together whipped cream cheese, milk, and minced garlic. In the bottom a pie pan, place a layer of zucchini covering the bottom the pan followed by a layer of tomato covering the zucchini. Spread half of the cream cheese mixture on top of the tomatoes. Top with 1/2 cup of Italian cheese blend. Place another layer of zucchini and tomatoes on top of cheese blend. Spread the remaining 1/2 of cream cheese mixture on top of zucchini and tomatoes. Top with 1/2 cup Italian cheese blend. Bake for 25 minutes.

MEXICAN CHARRO BEANS

INGREDIENTS

1 pound dried pinto beans

12 ounces bacon chopped

1 onion chopped

1 jalapeno chopped

4 garlic cloves minced

4 cups chicken broth

2 cups water

15 ounce can fire roasted tomatoes

1 tsp garlic powder

2 tsp chili powder

2 tsp cumin

Salt to taste

DIRECTIONS

Soak beans in water overnight or at least for 6 hours. Cook bacon in a large pot. Add in onions and jalapeno and cook for 5 minutes. Add garlic and stir for 30 seconds. Pour in beans, chicken broth, and water. Bring to boil, reduce heat, cover and simmer for 45 minutes. After 45 minutes, add in tomatoes, garlic powder, chili powder, and cumin. Add salt if needed. Cover and simmer for 30 more minutes.

JALAPENO POPPER PASTA SALAD

INGREDIENTS

5-6 jalapenos chopped and seeded

1 pound bacon

16 ounces of pasta

4 ounces cream cheese softened

1 cup mayo

1 cup sour cream

1 tsp garlic powder

1/2 tsp salt

1 cup shredded cheese

DIRECTIONS

Take the seeds out of the jalapenos and chop into small pieces. Cook the bacon and chop into pieces. Boil pasta as directed on box and rinse under cold water.
In a bowl, mix together cream cheese, mayo, sour cream, garlic, and salt.
Add in pasta, jalapenos, bacon and shredded cheese and mix.
Serve cold

GREEN CHILE RICE CASSEROLE

INGREDIENTS

4 cups cooked rice

1 cup sour cream

8 ounces green chiles

1/2 tsp garlic powder

1/2 tsp salt

1/2 tsp pepper

2 cup shredded cheese (save 1 cup to sprinkle on top)

DIRECTIONS

Preheat oven to 350 degrees. In a large bowl, mix together cooked rice, sour cream, green chiles, garlic powder, salt, pepper, and 1 cup shredded cheese. Pour mixture into a greased 9x13 inch pan. Top with 1 cup shredded cheese. Bake uncovered for 20 minutes.

Delicious DESSERTS

MINI PINEAPPLE UPSIDE DOWN BUNDT CAKES

Makes 12

These mini bundt cakes are the cutest dessert that you'll ever make! These are sweet and delicious and are bursting with flavor in every bite.

DIRECTIONS

Preheat oven to 350 degrees. Make the box of yellow cake mix as directed on box but substitute the water for pineapple juice. Melt the butter and brown sugar together in separate bowl. Spray the mini bundt pan with cooking spray. Scoop the butter and brown sugar mixture into the bottom of the mini bundt pan. Place a pineapple ring on top of the brown sugar and butter mixture. Place a Maraschino cherry in the pineapple hole. Pour the cake batter on top of the pineapple and cherry, filling the mini Bundt cups 3/4 full. Bake for 25 minutes. Let cool before removing from pan.

INGREDIENTS

1 box of Yellow cake mix along with the ingredients it calls for (eggs and oil)

You will substitute the water for pineapple juice

1 (15 ounce) can pineapple rings

12 Maraschino cherries

1 stick of butter

1 cup brown sugar

CHOCOLATE MOCHA SALTED CARAMEL CAKE

DIRECTIONS

Preheat oven to 350 degrees. Mix the cake mix, box of pudding, vegetable oil. sour cream, and eggs until combined. Pour in the brewed coffee and mix with a mixer for 1 minute. Spray bundt pan with cooking spray and pour cake mixture into bundt pan. Bake for 55-60 minutes.

Chocolate ganache: Add heavy cream to a pan and bring to a boil. Remove from heat and add in semi sweet chocolate chips. Stir in chocolate chips then cover with lid. Let sit for 5 minutes. After 5 minutes, use a whisk and whisk until smooth. Let cool for 10-15 minutes.

Salted caramel drizzle: Place caramel bits and heavy cream in pan. Cook on low until caramel is melted. Add in salt and stir.

Once the bundt cake is completely cooled, pour the chocolate ganache over the cake. Then drizzle the salted caramel over the ganache.

INGREDIENTS

For cake:
1 box chocolate cake mix
1 box chocolate instant pudding mix (3.9 ounces)
1/2 cup vegetable oil
1 cup sour cream
4 eggs
1 cup of brewed coffee

Chocolate Ganache
3/4 cup heavy cream
8 ounces semi sweet chocolate chips

Salted Caramel Drizzle
15 pieces of caramel baking bits
2 Tbs heavy cream
1 tsp salt

EASY MINI CHEESECAKES

Makes 18

DIRECTIONS

For the crust: Mix together the graham cracker crumbs, sugar, and melted butter. Place cupcake liners in the muffin tin and place graham cracker mixture in the bottom of the liners. Press down with a spoon.

Cheesecake filling: Beat the cream cheese and sugar until smooth. Add in the eggs, sour, cream and vanilla and mix.

Pour the cheesecake mixture into the cupcake liners. Fill the cups 3/4 full. Bake at 350 degrees for 17-19 minutes. After they have baked, let them cool completely. Top with cherry pie filling. Refrigerate.

INGREDIENTS

Pie Crust:

1 1/2 cups graham cracker crumbs

2 Tbs sugar

4 Tbs melted butter

Cheesecake filling:

16 ounces cream cheese softened

1/2 cup sugar

2 eggs

1/2 cup sour cream

1 tsp vanilla

Cherry pie filling for topping

PECAN PIE BROWNIES

INGREDIENTS

Box brownie mix plus ingredients needed for brownie mix

Pecan pie topping:

4 eggs

1/2 cup butter

1 cup sugar

1 1/2 cup light corn syrup

1 teaspoon vanilla

3 cups whole pecans

DIRECTIONS

Preheat oven to 350 degrees. Mix brownie mix as directed on back of the box. Pour into a 9X13 inch pan. Bake for 20 minutes. While the brownies bake, in a pan mix butter, sugar, light corn syrup, and vanilla. Before it heats up, mix in the 4 eggs. Cook on medium heat and bring to a simmer. Whisk constantly for 15 minutes. After whisking for 15 minutes, remove from heat. Add in 3 cups of pecans. Fold in with a rubber spatula. Pour pecans over brownies. Bake for 25 more minutes.

CHERRY CREAM CHEESE PUFF PASTRY BRAID

Makes 2 pastries

DIRECTIONS

Preheat oven to 375 degrees. Lay out both thawed puff pastry sheets onto parchment paper. Mix together cream cheese, powdered sugar, lemon juice, and vanilla in a bowl until smooth. Divide the cream cheese mixture evenly onto each puff pastry and spread a layer down the center. Spoon the cherry pie filling on top of the cream cheese mixture. Cut strips along the sides of the puff pastry on each side of the mixture. Fold the strips over the cream cheese and cherry mixture crossing the strips over each other to make the braid. Brush egg white on top of the puff pastry and sprinkle with sugar. Bake for 30 minutes.

INGREDIENTS

1 box puff pastry sheets (2 puff pastry sheets inside box)

8 ounces of cream cheese

1/2 cup powdered sugar

1 Tbs lemon juice

1/2 tsp vanilla extract

1 can cherry pie filling

1 egg white

1 tsp sugar

94

COWBOY COOKIES

INGREDIENTS

1 cup butter

1 1/2 cup brown sugar

1/2 cup white sugar

2 eggs

2 teaspoons vanilla

2 1/2 cups flour

1 tsp baking soda

1 tsp cinnamon

1/2 tsp salt

2 cups oats

3/4 cups shredded coconut

1/2 cup chopped pecans

12 ounces chocolate chips

DIRECTIONS

Preheat oven to 350 degrees. Beat butter, brown sugar, sugar, eggs, and vanilla until smooth. In a separate bowl, mix flour, baking soda, cinnamon, and salt. Add in oats, shredded coconut, pecans, and chocolate chips. Mix together. Add the dry ingredients into the wet ingredients. Stir until combined. Form into 1 inch balls and press down lightly. Bake on greased cookie sheet for 14 minutes.

95

ORANGE CRANBERRY BREAD

INGREDIENTS

3/4 cup orange juice

2 Tbs orange zest

1 egg

2 Tbs vegetable oil

2 cups of flour

3/4 cup sugar

1 1/2 tsp baking powder

1/4 tsp salt

1 cup dried cranberries

Orange glaze:
1 cup powdered sugar

2 Tbs orange juice

1/2 tsp vanilla

DIRECTIONS

Preheat oven to 350 degrees. Mix flour, sugar, baking powder, and salt. In a separate bowl, mix orange juice, orange zest, egg, and vegetable oil. Mix the wet ingredients with the dry ingredients. Stir gently until combined. Fold in 1 cup dried cranberries. Pour batter into a greased loaf pan. Bake for 50-55 minutes. Mix ingredients for the orange glaze and pour over the cool loaf of bread.

5 INGREDIENT BROWNIES

This brownie recipe is simple yet delicious. You can whip these up in no time to satisfy your sweet tooth.

DIRECTIONS

Preheat oven to 350 degrees. Line a 9x9 inch pan with parchment paper. In a bowl, melt butter and whisk in sugar and eggs. Stir in flour and cocoa powder and smooth. Pour into pan and bake for 35-40 minutes.

INGREDIENTS

1 cup butter melted

2 cups sugar

4 eggs

1 cup flour

2/3 cup cocoa powder

CARROT CAKE CUPCAKES

Makes 18

INGREDIENTS

1 1/2 cups finely grated carrots

1 1/4 cup flour

1 tsp baking soda

1/2 tsp baking powder

1/2 tsp cinnamon

1/2 tsp nutmeg

1/4 tsp ground ginger

1/2 cup veg oil

1/2 cup brown sugar

1/3 cup sugar

2 eggs

1 tsp vanilla

Icing:
8 ounces cream cheese

1 stick butter

3 cups powdered sugar

1/2 tsp vanilla

Chopped walnuts

DIRECTIONS

Preheat oven to 350 degrees. In a bowl, mix together flour, baking soda, baking powder, cinnamon, nutmeg, and ground ginger. Set aside. In a large bowl, mix oil, brown sugar, sugar, eggs, and vanilla. Add in sour cream and grated carrots. Mix until combined. Next, add in the dry ingredients and mix. Spoon into cupcakes liners in muffin tin, filling 3/4 of the way full. Bake for 18 minutes. For Icing, beat the cream cheese, butter, powdered sugar, and vanilla and smooth. Spread on top of cooled cupcakes and top with walnuts.

LEMON BLUBERRY TRIFLE

INGREDIENTS

2 (3.4 ounce) boxes lemon pudding mix

3 cups whole milk

1 tsp lemon zest

Whipped Cream:

1 cup heavy cream

1/4 cup powdered sugar

1/2 tsp vanilla

14 ounce Angel Food cake

2 pints blueberries

DIRECTIONS

Whisk together the lemon pudding mix, whole milk, and lemon zest. In a separate bowl, beat together the heavy cream, powdered sugar, and vanilla until soft peaks form. Cut the Angel Food cake into cubes. In the serving bowl, place a layer of Angel Food cake in the bottom. Pour 1/3 of the pudding mixture over the cake. Add 1/3 of the blueberries. Repeat this 2 more times for a total of 3 layers. Top with remaining whipped cream. Refrigerate for 2-4 hours.

CHOCOLATE CHIP BANANA BREAD

INGREDIENTS

3 ripe bananas

1 cup brown sugar

2 eggs

2 Tbs sour cream

1/4 cup vegetable oil

1/2 tsp vanilla

1 3/4 cup flour

1 tsp baking soda

1/2 tsp baking powder

1/2 tsp cinnamon

1 cup semi sweet chocolate chips

DIRECTIONS

Preheat oven to 350 degrees. In a bowl, mash the ripe bananas. Add in brown sugar, eggs, sour cream, oil, and vanilla and mix. Stir in flour, baking soda, baking powder, and cinnamon. Fold in chocolate chips. Pour into a greased loaf pan. Bake for 50-55 minutes.

DIDI'S ORANGE CAKE

INGREDIENTS

2 1/2 cups flour

1 3/4 cup sugar

1 1/2 tsp baking soda

1 tsp baking powder

1/2 tsp salt

1 cup vegetable oil

1 cup orange juice

3 eggs

1 cup sour cream

2 tsp orange zest

Frosting:

1 cup butter softened

8 ounces cream cheese softened

4 cups powder sugar

1 tsp orange zest

2 Tbs orange juice

DIRECTIONS

Preheat oven to 350 degrees. Mix together flour, sugar, baking soda, baking powder, and salt. In a separate bowl, beat together oil, orange juice, eggs, sour cream, and orange zest. Slowly add the dry ingredients into the wet ingredients and mix until combined. Pour batter into 2 9x9 inch greased pans and bake for 25-30 minutes. For Frosting: Beat together butter, cream cheese, orange juice, and orange zest. Add in powdered sugar one cup at a time and mix. Frost the cake once cake has completely cooled.

MISSISSIPPI MUD BROWNIES

DIRECTIONS

Preheat oven to 350 degrees. Beat the butter and sugar together. Mix in cocoa powder, oil, eggs, and vanilla. Pour batter into a greased 9X13 inch pan. Bake for 25-30 minutes. Add the mini marshmallows on top of the cooked brownies and bake another 5 minutes. For the Frosting: Beat together evaporated milk, melted butter, cocoa powder, and vanilla. Add in powdered sugar 1 cup at a time and mix. Spread the frosting on top of the cooled brownies.

INGREDIENTS

2 1/2 cup butter softened

1/3 cup cocoa powder

2 cups sugar

1 1/2 cup flour

4 eggs

1/2 cup vegetable oil

2 tsp vanilla

3 cups mini marshmallows

Frosting:
1/3 cup cocoa powder

1/3 cup evaporated milk

1/2 cup melted butter

3 cups powdered sugar

1 tsp vanilla

EASY LEMON CREAM PIE

INGREDIENTS

2 (14 ounce) cans sweetened condensed milk

1/2 cup sour cream

3/4 cup lemon juice

1 Tbs lemon zest

1 cup heavy cream

1/4 cup powdered sugar

9 inch Graham cracker pie crust

DIRECTIONS

Preheat oven to 350 degrees. Mix together the sweetened condensed milk and the sour cream. Add in the lemon juice and lemon zest and mix. Pour pie filling into pie crust and bake for 9 minutes. Let pie cool completely. For whipped cream topping: Whisk together heavy cream and powdered sugar until stiff peaks form. Top the pie with whipped cream. Refrigerate.

THANK YOU

I hope you've enjoyed my cookbook and that my recipes have brought joy to you and your family.